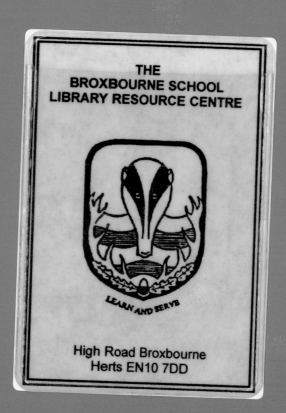

Frontiers of
Medicine

CONTENTS

Designed and produced by
NW Books Ltd,
28 Percy Street
London, W1P 9FF

Design David West
Children's Book Design
Designer Flick Killerby
Editor Roger Vlitos
Researcher Emma Krikler
Consultant Jane Thomas
Illustrator Aziz Khan

First published in
Great Britain in 1991 by
Franklin Watts, 96 Leonard St
London EC2A 4RH

A CIP catalogue record for
this book is available from
the British Library.

ISBN 0-7496-0588-X

Printed in Belgium

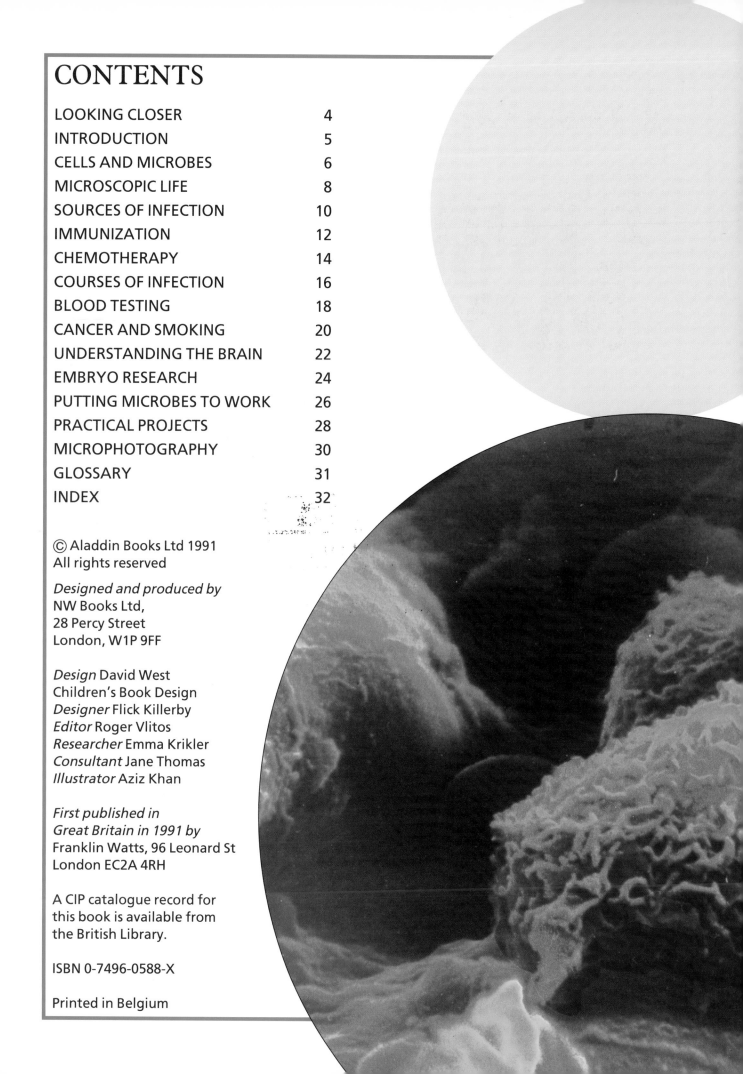

THROUGH · THE · MICROSCOPE

Frontiers of Medicine

Lionel Bender

FRANKLIN WATTS
London: New York: Toronto: Sydney

LOOKING CLOSER

Microscopes and magnifying glasses work by using lenses and light. A lens is usually a thin, circular glass, thicker in the middle, which bends rays of light so that when you look through it an object appears enlarged. A microscope uses several lenses. It will also have a set of adjustments to give you a choice over how much you want to magnify.

When we want to view something under a microscope it must be small enough to fit on a glass slide. This is put on the stage over the mirror and light is reflected through so that the lenses inside can magnify the view for us. But not all microscopes work this way. The greatest detail can be seen with an electron microscope which uses electron beams and electromagnets.

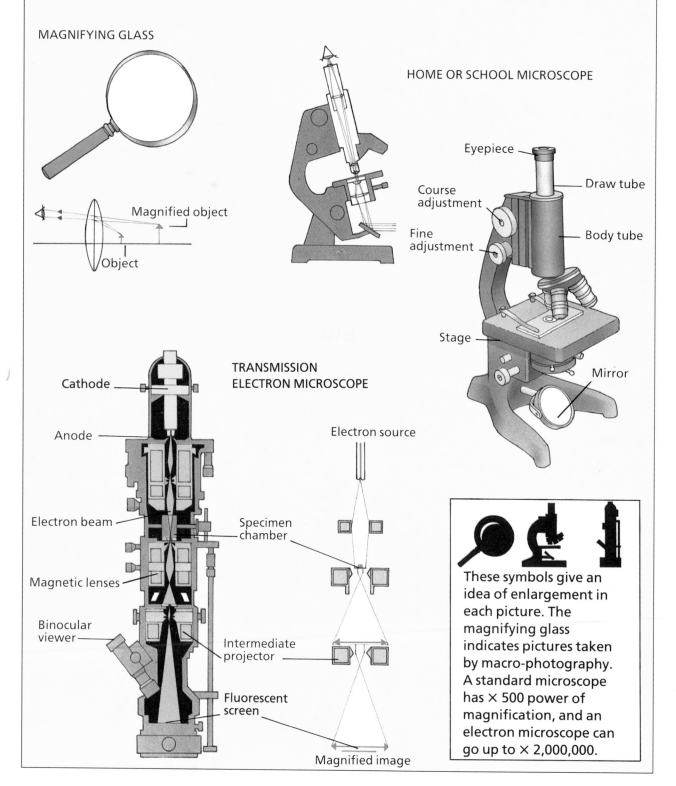

MAGNIFYING GLASS

Magnified object

Object

HOME OR SCHOOL MICROSCOPE

Eyepiece

Draw tube

Course adjustment

Fine adjustment

Body tube

Stage

Mirror

TRANSMISSION ELECTRON MICROSCOPE

Cathode

Anode

Electron beam

Magnetic lenses

Binocular viewer

Specimen chamber

Intermediate projector

Fluorescent screen

Electron source

Magnified image

These symbols give an idea of enlargement in each picture. The magnifying glass indicates pictures taken by macro-photography. A standard microscope has × 500 power of magnification, and an electron microscope can go up to × 2,000,000.

INTRODUCTION

A microscope is used to study things too small to be seen with the naked eye. This book has pictures taken through different types of microscope, or with special magnifying lenses attached to cameras. Next to each picture is a symbol showing how each was made. This will give you an idea of the number of times (written ×) the objects are magnified. Diagrams are used to help explain what the microscopes are showing us, or to illustrate scientific equipment and experiments.

The science of medicine often involves the study of cells, the tiny building units of living things, and comparing those affected by disease or injury with those of the healthy body. In this book we look at how microscopes have helped us to understand our bodies and the nature of illness. Microscopes have played an important role in finding the causes and cures of various disorders. More than any other tool, microscopes have helped to push forward the frontiers of Medicine.

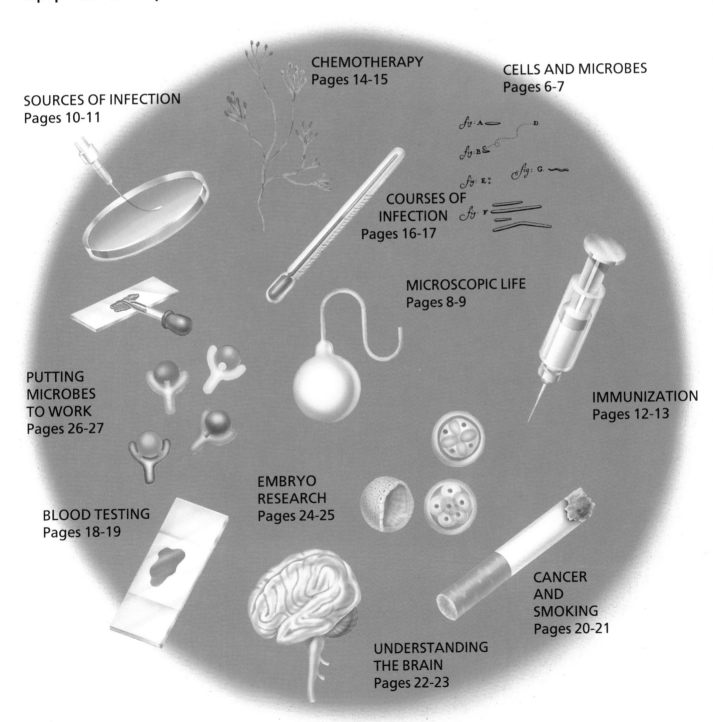

CHEMOTHERAPY
Pages 14-15

CELLS AND MICROBES
Pages 6-7

SOURCES OF INFECTION
Pages 10-11

COURSES OF
INFECTION
Pages 16-17

MICROSCOPIC LIFE
Pages 8-9

PUTTING
MICROBES
TO WORK
Pages 26-27

IMMUNIZATION
Pages 12-13

EMBRYO
RESEARCH
Pages 24-25

BLOOD TESTING
Pages 18-19

CANCER
AND
SMOKING
Pages 20-21

UNDERSTANDING
THE BRAIN
Pages 22-23

fig: A

fig: B

D

fig: E:

fig: F

fig: G.

CELLS AND MICROBES

The foundations of modern medicine were laid in ancient Greece, when Hippocrates (460-377 BC) developed a system called "diagnosis". This is the way that doctors use examination and reason to decide what is wrong with a patient. But it was not until a Dutchman named Antonie van Leeuwenhoek (1632-1723) studied tiny creatures from his mouth with a single-lens microscope that microbes, some of which cause diseases, were recorded (see diagram on left). Soon afterwards, an Englishman, Robert Hooke (1635-1703), used more elaborate microscopes to prove that all living things are made up of tiny cells; and an Italian, Marcello Malpighi (1629-64), made the first microscopic studies of human body organs.

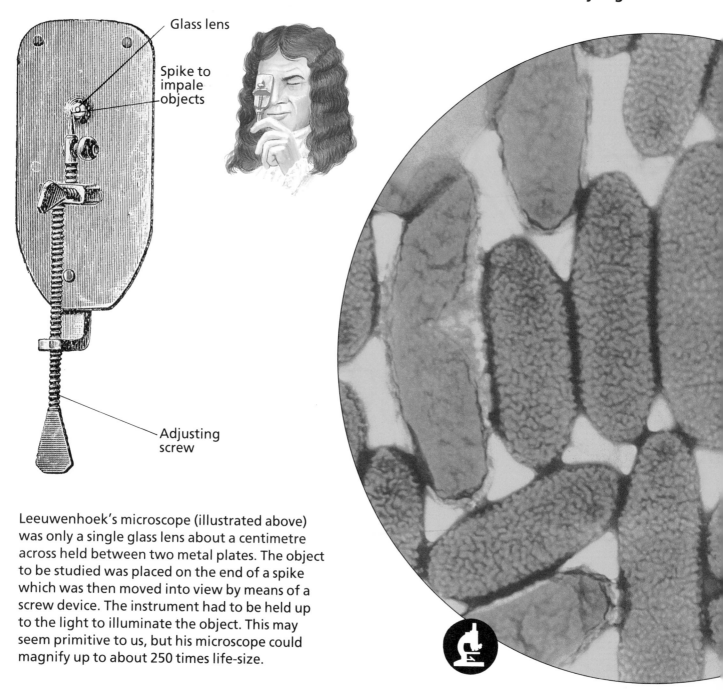

Glass lens

Spike to impale objects

Adjusting screw

Leeuwenhoek's microscope (illustrated above) was only a single glass lens about a centimetre across held between two metal plates. The object to be studied was placed on the end of a spike which was then moved into view by means of a screw device. The instrument had to be held up to the light to illuminate the object. This may seem primitive to us, but his microscope could magnify up to about 250 times life-size.

Antonie van Leeuwenhoek was one of the first people to make a microscopic study of the everyday world. The photo below-left shows the cells of a fern plant seen through a modern copy of Leeuwenhoek's simple microscope.

Robert Hooke studied plant cells and tiny bacteria like those in the photo below-right, magnified × 5,270. The bacteria shown here cause Legionnaires' disease. However, neither Leeuwenhoek nor Hooke realized the importance of their observations to medical science.

Robert Hooke's "compound" microscope (below) had three lenses. A "condenser" concentrated light onto the object, which was magnified by a small "objective" lens. The magnified image was viewed with the "eyepiece" lens.

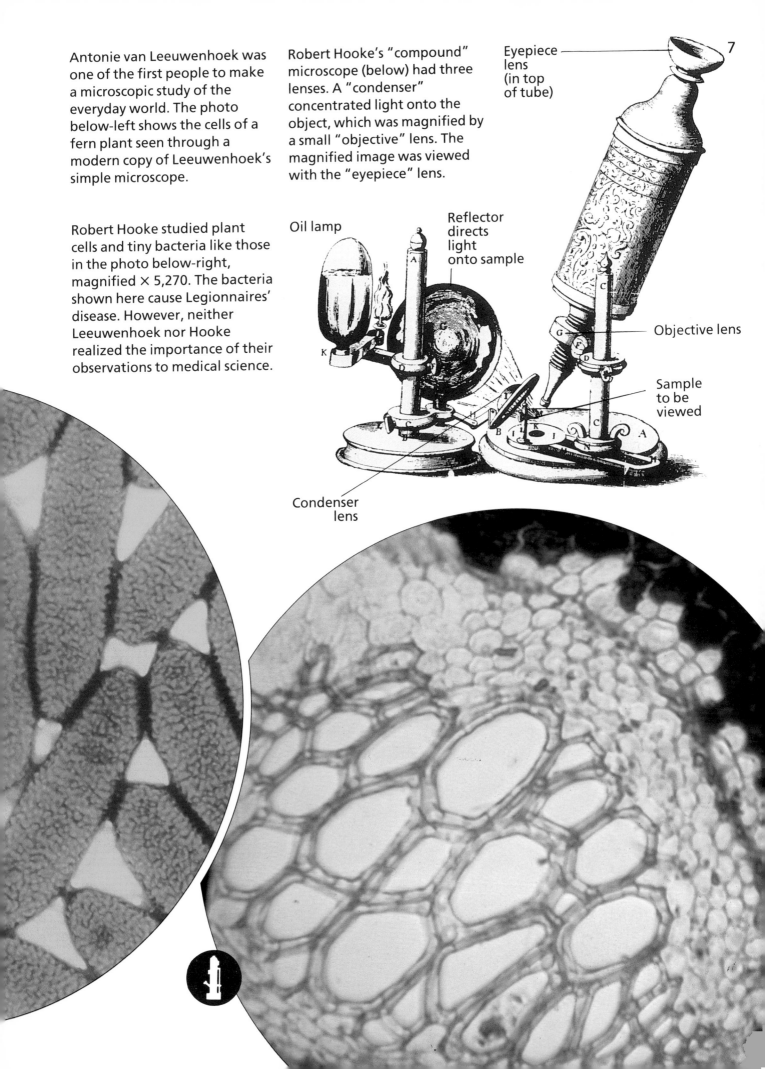

Eyepiece lens (in top of tube)

Objective lens

Sample to be viewed

Reflector directs light onto sample

Oil lamp

Condenser lens

7

MICROSCOPIC LIFE

For over 100 years after the discoveries made with the first microscopes, people still believed that small creatures just sprang to life in soil, air or water. So it was thought that maggots, one stage in the life-cycle of House flies, simply grew out of meat. It took the great French scientist Louis Pasteur (1822-1895) to confirm that tiny living things come from existing ones. He did this by heating broth, which bacteria would normally have spoiled within a few days, inside a "gooseneck" flask (see diagram left). The heat killed off any bacteria, and the shape of the neck prevented any new ones from entering in the air. A similar process, called pasteurization, is still used to kill harmful bacteria in the milk we drink.

The life-cycle of the House fly (illustrated right) was first established by an Italian called Francesco Redi (1626-1697). He proved that the adult flies laid microscopic eggs in meat and that maggots (magnified ×3,000 below) hatch from them.

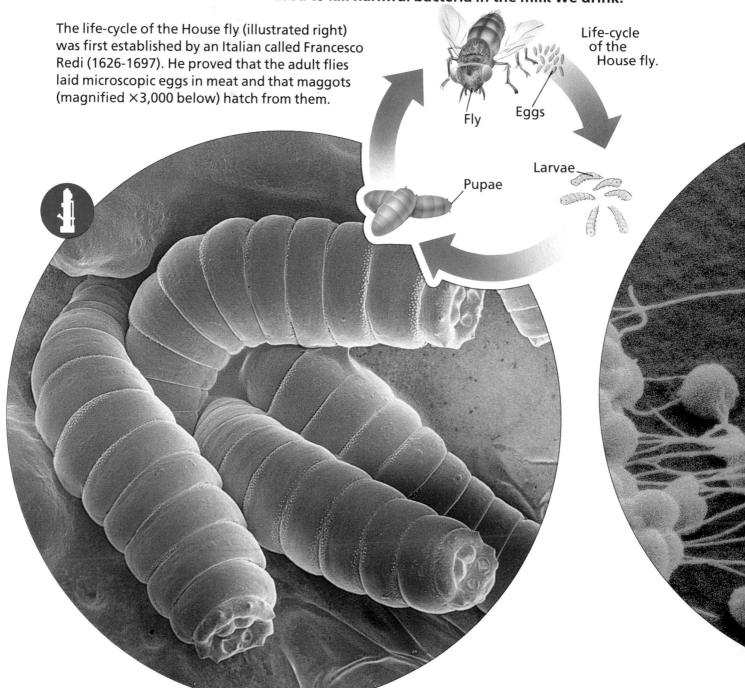

Life-cycle of the House fly.

Fly

Eggs

Larvae

Pupae

In medical laboratories where the cause of a disease is sought, saliva, urine or blood from the patient is spread on a layer of food material in a glass or plastic dish. The food and dish are first sterilized (heated to a high temperature to kill all microbes) and allowed to cool. The chosen body fluid is then placed on the food, where any bacteria present grow, multiply in their millions, and form colonies like those on the right. The bacteria shown here cause the disease anthrax. If no bacteria are put on the food and no air – which may carry bacteria – is allowed to enter the dish, no colonies appear.

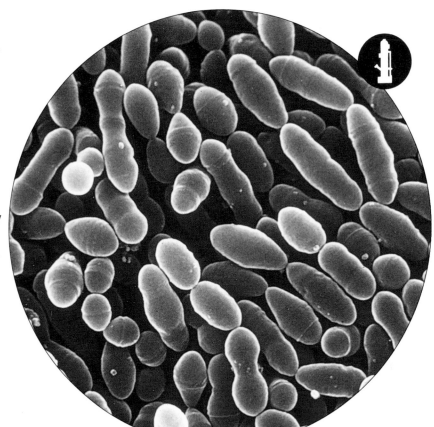

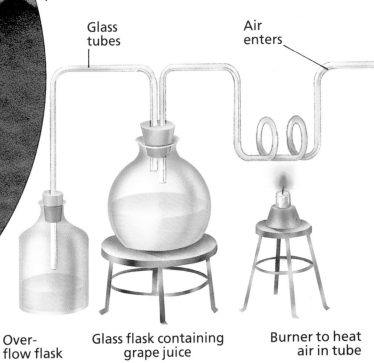

A German scientist, Theodor Schwann (1810-1882), used the experiment below to prove that air would not cause fermentation in grape juice all by itself. His microscope showed that the growth of tiny yeast cells in the juice caused fermentation. Louis Pasteur used a similar experiment to show that bacteria exist in the air. The bacteria shown left ($\times$ 16,500) are often present in air and can cause throat infections.

Glass tubes

Air enters

Over-flow flask

Glass flask containing grape juice

Burner to heat air in tube

10

SOURCES OF INFECTION

In the 1790s an English doctor called Edward Jenner (1749-1823) experimented with inoculating people with a small quantity of cowpox virus in order to prevent infections of smallpox. However, like most people of his day, he never thought that microscopic creatures, which we call germs, were the cause of disease. Louis Pasteur was the first to prove their involvement. He also used a microscope to discover that some microbes survived by living in or on others. These creatures, known as parasites, can produce dangerous diseases such as anthrax, which kills people as well as other animals. Another example of a parasite is the rat-flea, which can carry the germs in its gut that cause bubonic plague.

Bacteria, which grow in colonies on food material (photo right), are just one type of microbe or micro-organism. Others include viruses, protozoa and some fungi and algae. "Germs" are disease-producing microbes. Viruses are tiny organisms which can only survive inside the cells of other creatures.

The photo in the centre shows the viruses responsible for the common cold seen under an electron microscope. The image below shows the bacterium *Treponema pallidum* (magnified × 8,700) which causes the disease known as syphilis.

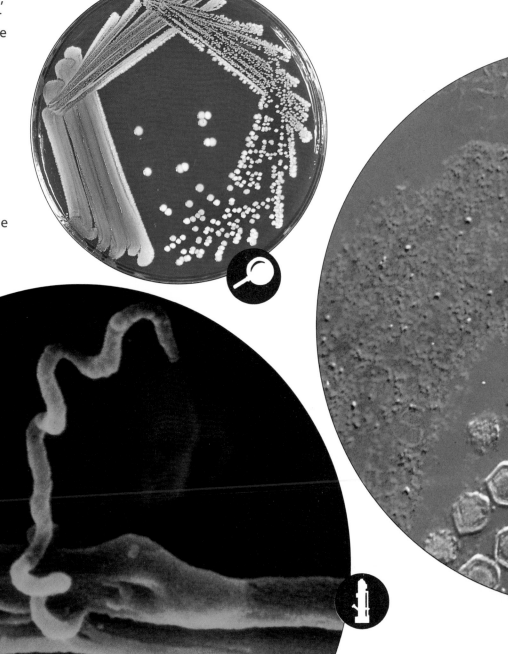

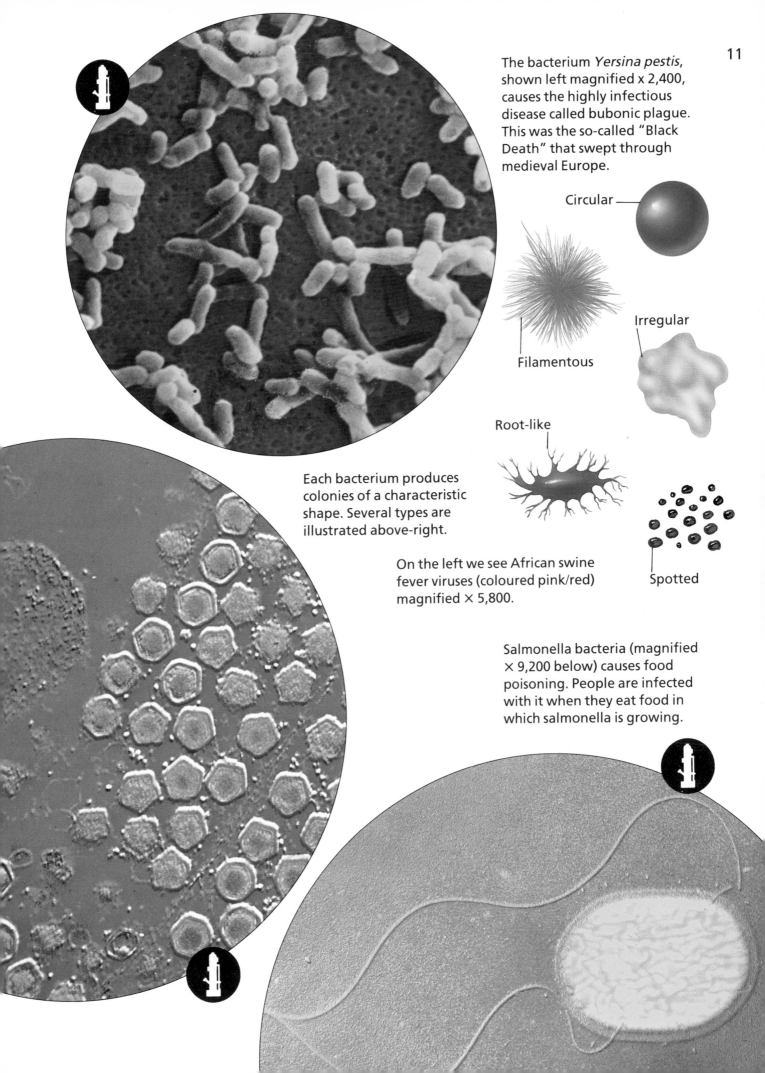

The bacterium *Yersina pestis*, shown left magnified x 2,400, causes the highly infectious disease called bubonic plague. This was the so-called "Black Death" that swept through medieval Europe.

Circular

Filamentous

Irregular

Root-like

Spotted

Each bacterium produces colonies of a characteristic shape. Several types are illustrated above-right.

On the left we see African swine fever viruses (coloured pink/red) magnified × 5,800.

Salmonella bacteria (magnified × 9,200 below) causes food poisoning. People are infected with it when they eat food in which salmonella is growing.

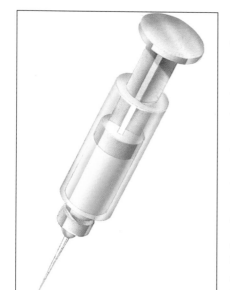

IMMUNIZATION

In spite of Pasteur's discovery of germs, 19th-century doctors were not sure why Edward Jenner's inoculations against smallpox worked. But they understood that the body has a natural defence, or "immune", system which can be improved. When a weak solution of a germ is injected into the body using a syringe (shown left) it gives the ability to combat the disease later on. This "immunization" was obvious even though microscopes at the time were not powerful enough to show the viruses. A German doctor called Robert Koch (1834-1910) made great progress in the battle against the diseases anthrax, cholera and tuberculosis. Koch grew their bacteria in his laboratory and proved how they caused the diseases.

Rabies shown left magnified x 36,700, is a deadly virus that spreads from animals to people.

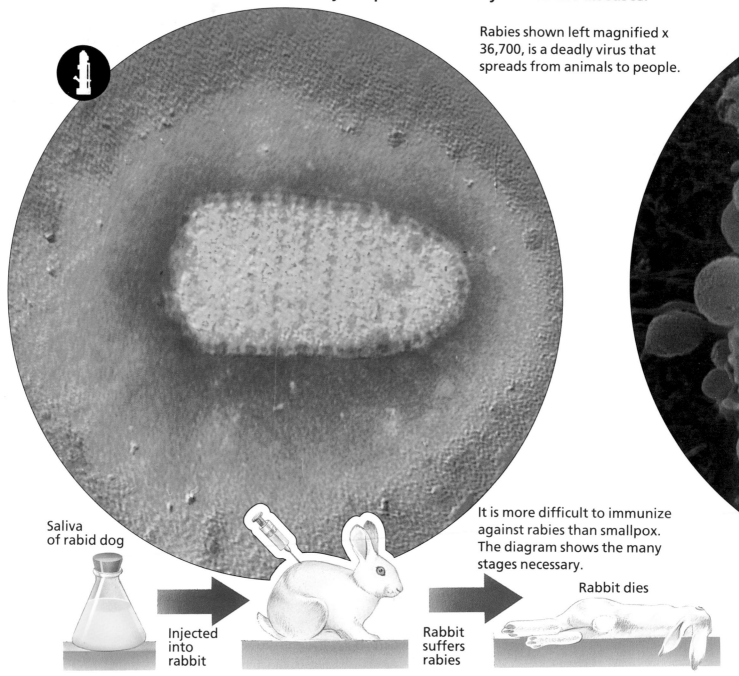

It is more difficult to immunize against rabies than smallpox. The diagram shows the many stages necessary.

Saliva of rabid dog

Injected into rabbit

Rabbit suffers rabies

Rabbit dies

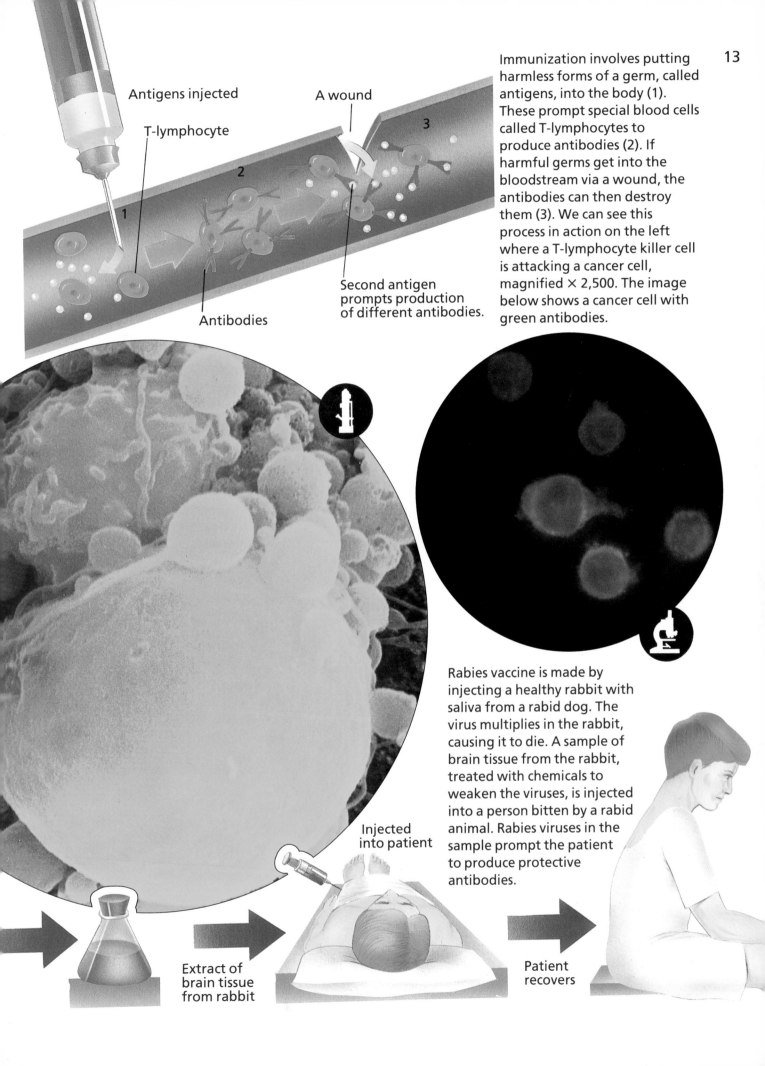

Antigens injected

T-lymphocyte

A wound

1   2   3

Antibodies

Second antigen prompts production of different antibodies.

Immunization involves putting harmless forms of a germ, called antigens, into the body (1). These prompt special blood cells called T-lymphocytes to produce antibodies (2). If harmful germs get into the bloodstream via a wound, the antibodies can then destroy them (3). We can see this process in action on the left where a T-lymphocyte killer cell is attacking a cancer cell, magnified × 2,500. The image below shows a cancer cell with green antibodies.

Rabies vaccine is made by injecting a healthy rabbit with saliva from a rabid dog. The virus multiplies in the rabbit, causing it to die. A sample of brain tissue from the rabbit, treated with chemicals to weaken the viruses, is injected into a person bitten by a rabid animal. Rabies viruses in the sample prompt the patient to produce protective antibodies.

Injected into patient

Extract of brain tissue from rabbit

Patient recovers

CHEMOTHERAPY

Chemotherapy, the treatment of diseases with chemicals, began in the 1900s. Scientists discovered the bacteria which causes tetanus, typhoid and syphilis and looked for ways of destroying germs in patients without harming healthy tissues and organs. In 1910, German scientist Paul Ehrlich (1854-1915) made the first such "magic bullet", Salvarsan, a chemical that kills the bacteria causing syphilis. In 1928, Scottish scientist Alexander Fleming (1881-1955) accidentally discovered an antibiotic – a chemical produced by one type of microbe that destroys others – when he noticed that a fungus, *Penicillium* (shown left), had contaminated samples of bacteria grown on dishes and killed the bacteria.

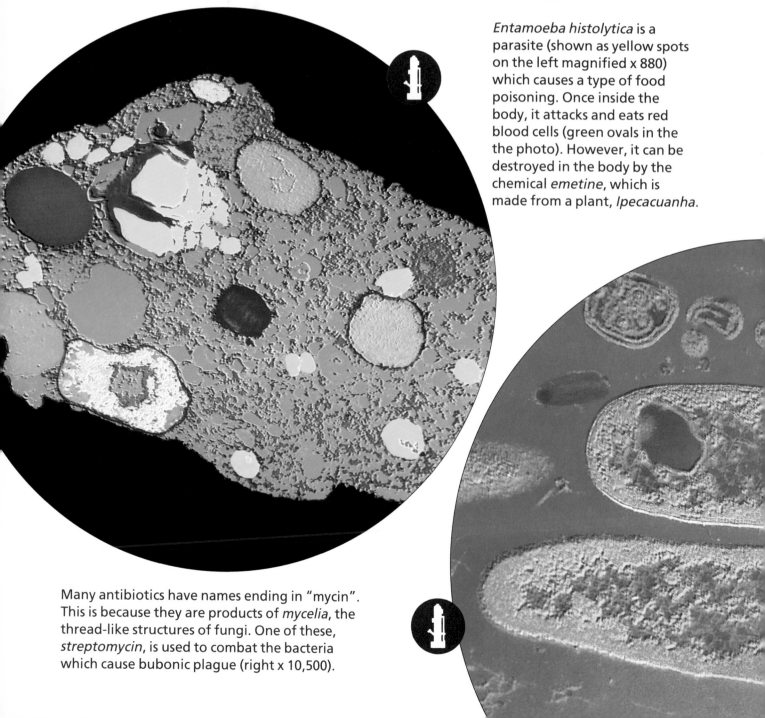

Entamoeba histolytica is a parasite (shown as yellow spots on the left magnified x 880) which causes a type of food poisoning. Once inside the body, it attacks and eats red blood cells (green ovals in the the photo). However, it can be destroyed in the body by the chemical *emetine*, which is made from a plant, *Ipecacuanha*.

Many antibiotics have names ending in "mycin". This is because they are products of *mycelia*, the thread-like structures of fungi. One of these, *streptomycin*, is used to combat the bacteria which cause bubonic plague (right x 10,500).

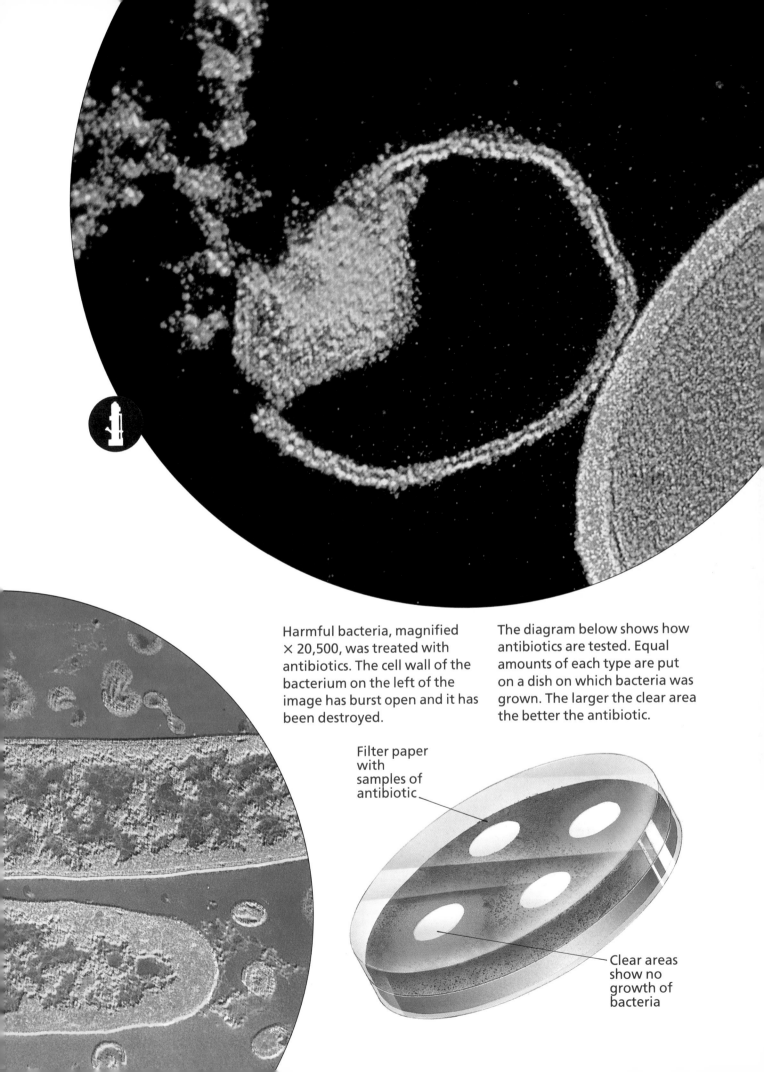

Harmful bacteria, magnified × 20,500, was treated with antibiotics. The cell wall of the bacterium on the left of the image has burst open and it has been destroyed.

The diagram below shows how antibiotics are tested. Equal amounts of each type are put on a dish on which bacteria was grown. The larger the clear area the better the antibiotic.

Filter paper with samples of antibiotic

Clear areas show no growth of bacteria

COURSES OF INFECTION

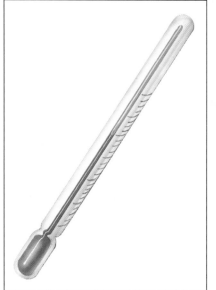

As the diagram below shows, germs can enter the body in a variety of everyday ways. Once inside, they may grow and multiply. For the first few hours or days of infection the person shows no symptoms (signs) of the disease. Then, as the microbes reach high numbers and produce more of their own chemicals, the person could develop a high temperature, headache, upset stomach and so on. The body's natural defences combat the germs and usually overcome them after a few days; but sometimes the microbes can go on to cause serious harm. Using a thermometer, a doctor can check how well the body's natural defences, or the medicines which have been taken, are keeping down the patients's temperature.

The protozoan in the photo on the left, magnified × 1190 and coloured green, enters the body with food. It attaches itself to the inside of the intestines and can cause a nasty stomachache.

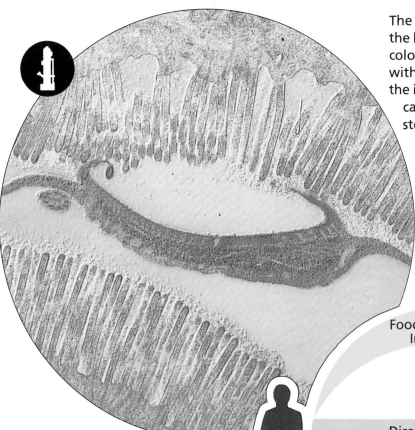

Food and water –
Indirect

Direct contact –
Touching, kissing and sneezing

Insects and microscopic organisms

Infected person

Healthy person

Animal source

The diagram right shows the three main ways in which disease-causing microbes pass from an infected person to a healthy one. It also shows how diseases pass from wild animals to people. Diseases transmitted, or passed on, in food and water include cholera and salmonella. Some microbes multiply within insects and are passed on. Others are carried on the insect's body.

The fungus *Tinea capitis*, shown right × 580, causes ringworm, an infection of the scalp. It spreads easily from an infected person to someone else if combs or towels are shared.

The rat-flea (× 20 below) can carry bubonic plague. If an infected flea bites a person to suck blood, the plague microbe will enter the bloodstream. This results in fever, sickness, ulcers, and perhaps even death.

Sleeping sickness is a tropical disease carried by the tsetse fly. The insect injects the germs (right) into a person's bloodstream.

BLOOD TESTING

Blood testing is used to search for the cause of a disease, or determine the correct type of blood for transfusions. Transfusions are needed to give blood to a sick person or to one who has lost blood due to an injury or during surgery. The donor's and the recipient's blood must match. To look for microbes in blood, a small sample – from a pin-prick – is smeared on to a microscope slide, as shown left. Doctors may then be able to see the protozoan responsible for malaria or the bacterium causing typhoid. They may also find clues about a patient's ill health. For example, a low number of red blood cells shows the patient may be suffering from lack of vitamin B or iron in their diet.

White blood cells ×3,450 (coloured dark-blue in the computer image below) travel in the bloodstream. They gobble up invading microbes and produce antibodies.

A healthy person has up to 10,000 white cells in each cubic millimetre of blood. A person with leukaemia, a cancer of the blood, may have up to 600,000.

Red blood cells (× 1,000 below) carry chemicals on their surface that act like antigens (see page 13). In the normal ABO blood groups each serum, or blood fluid, is different. Some possess antibodies against the antigens but others do not. The test for blood grouping is recorded in the diagram on the right. If a blood sample tested with anti-A serum results in blood cells clumping, person is group A, and so on with each group.

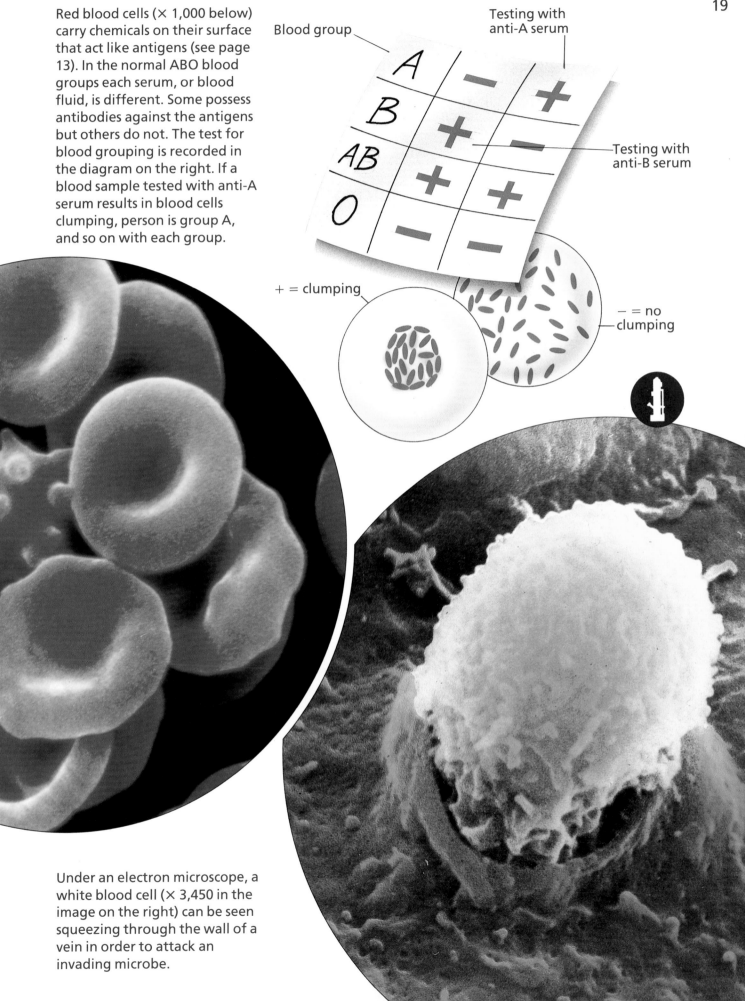

Blood group

Testing with anti-A serum

Testing with anti-B serum

	Testing with anti-A serum	Testing with anti-B serum
A	−	+
B	+	−
AB	+	+
O	−	−

+ = clumping

− = no clumping

Under an electron microscope, a white blood cell (× 3,450 in the image on the right) can be seen squeezing through the wall of a vein in order to attack an invading microbe.

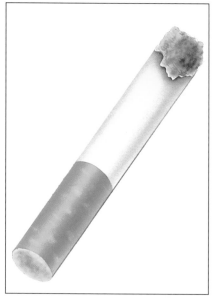

CANCER AND SMOKING

Cancer cells are cells which were once healthy but have become abnormal and grow rapidly, causing damage. As well as lung cancer, there are cancers of the skin, stomach, blood and so on. Smoking tobacco is partly responsible for a wide range of serious illnesses including cancer. Microscopic studies of diseased lungs, heart and blood vessels have proved this time after time. Tobacco smoke contains poisonous chemicals, some of which can cause cancer. Smoking also produces large amounts of tar. This consists of millions of dust-like particles which stick to and irritate the linings of the breathing tubes. Tar also clogs the delicate air-sacs within the lungs, which makes breathing difficult and puts a strain on the heart.

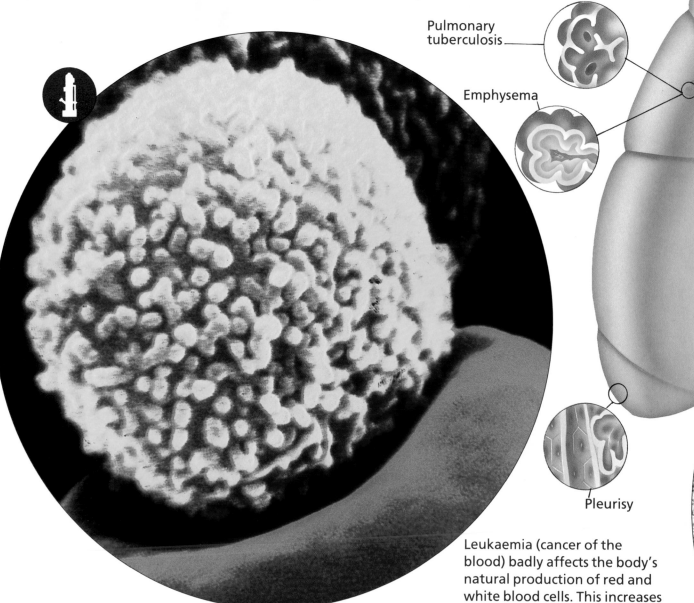

Pulmonary tuberculosis

Emphysema

Pleurisy

The white cell in the image above, seen here × 4,860, is from a person with leukaemia.

The diseased cell has lots of tiny surface projections not present on healthy white cells.

Leukaemia (cancer of the blood) badly affects the body's natural production of red and white blood cells. This increases the chances that microbes will invade the person. They will then be able to multiply, which can cause other diseases.

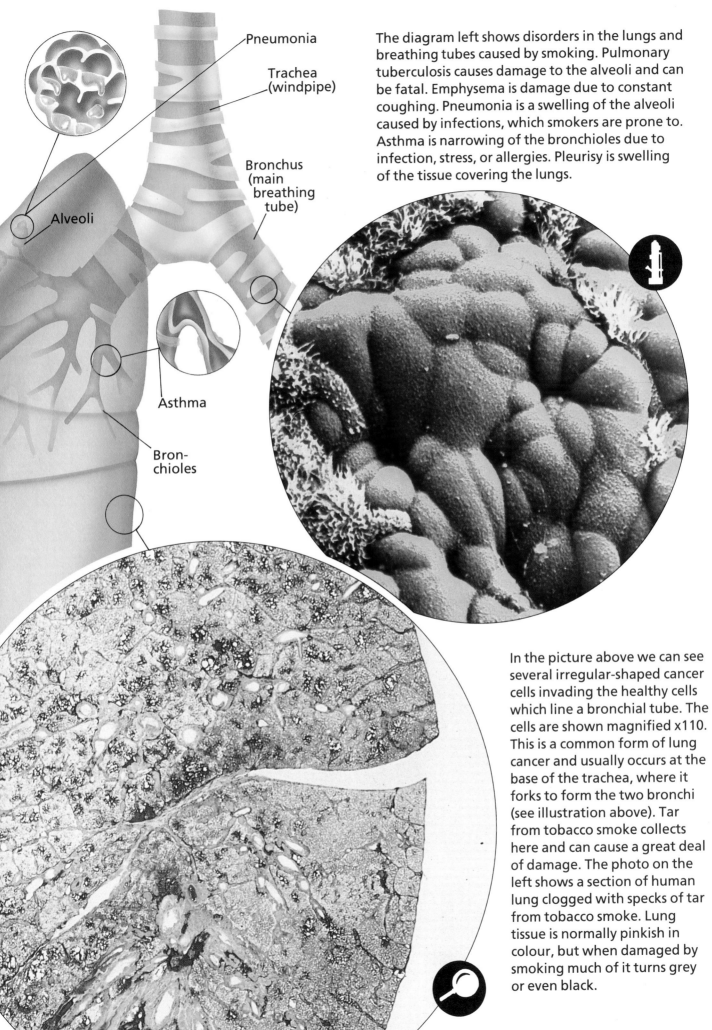

Pneumonia

Trachea
(windpipe)

Bronchus
(main
breathing
tube)

Alveoli

Asthma

Bron-
chioles

The diagram left shows disorders in the lungs and breathing tubes caused by smoking. Pulmonary tuberculosis causes damage to the alveoli and can be fatal. Emphysema is damage due to constant coughing. Pneumonia is a swelling of the alveoli caused by infections, which smokers are prone to. Asthma is narrowing of the bronchioles due to infection, stress, or allergies. Pleurisy is swelling of the tissue covering the lungs.

In the picture above we can see several irregular-shaped cancer cells invading the healthy cells which line a bronchial tube. The cells are shown magnified x110. This is a common form of lung cancer and usually occurs at the base of the trachea, where it forks to form the two bronchi (see illustration above). Tar from tobacco smoke collects here and can cause a great deal of damage. The photo on the left shows a section of human lung clogged with specks of tar from tobacco smoke. Lung tissue is normally pinkish in colour, but when damaged by smoking much of it turns grey or even black.

UNDERSTANDING THE BRAIN

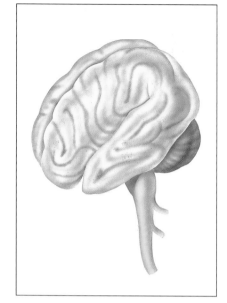

The microscope has also played an important role in discovering and understanding the detailed structure of the brain and how nerves carry millions of messages in between it and the rest of the body every second. Microscopic research has helped scientists and doctors understand how the brain can sometimes repair itself following injury; and also how it can be affected by various medicines and drugs. The brain is the body's control centre. It functions like a computer, collecting information from sense organs – the eyes, ears, nose, tongue and skin – sorting the information, then sending out signals to muscles and other tissues and to organs such as the heart, lungs, liver, kidneys, nose and eyes.

Nerve cells in the brain are magnified × 160 below. Each is connected to the others by thousands of branch-like dendrites. A finger-like fibre, the axon, is also visible in each.

The spinal cord carries messages to and from the brain from muscles and organs all over the body. The picture above – a cross-section of part of a normal spinal cord × 20 – shows the two main areas of nerve cells. The "white matter" at the top is made up of nerve fibres. "Grey matter" at the bottom (here stained orange to make it stand out) contains nerve cell bodies.

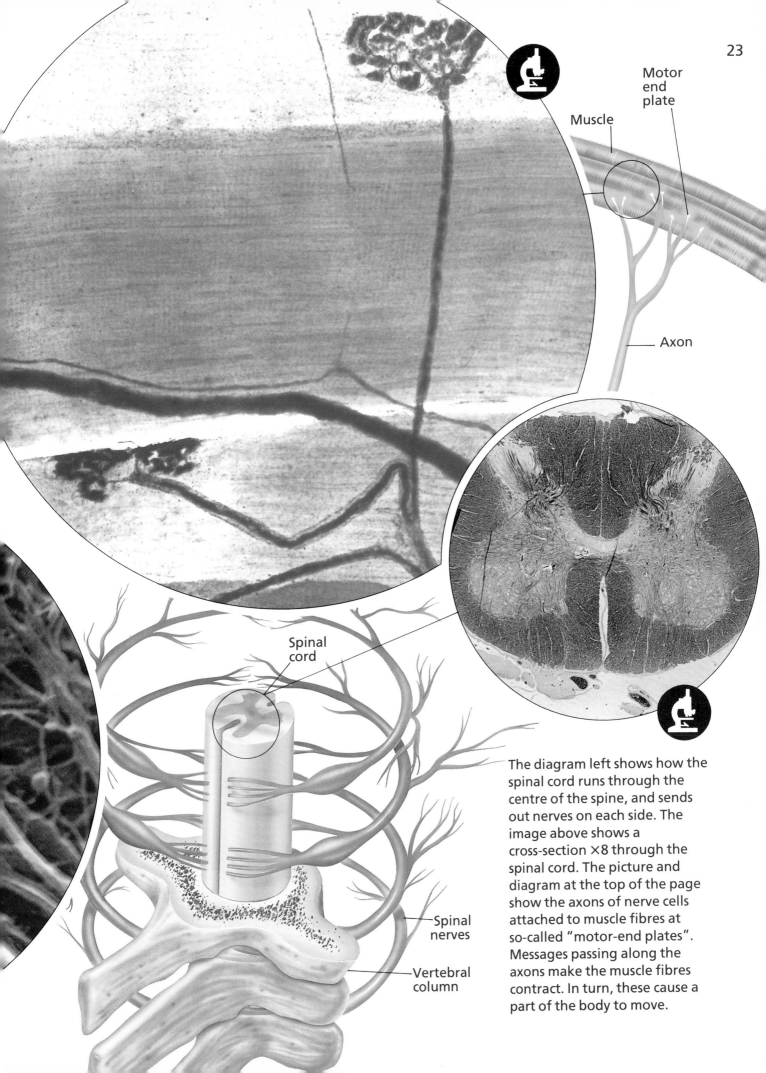

Motor
end
plate

Muscle

Axon

Spinal
cord

Spinal
nerves

Vertebral
column

The diagram left shows how the
spinal cord runs through the
centre of the spine, and sends
out nerves on each side. The
image above shows a
cross-section ×8 through the
spinal cord. The picture and
diagram at the top of the page
show the axons of nerve cells
attached to muscle fibres at
so-called "motor-end plates".
Messages passing along the
axons make the muscle fibres
contract. In turn, these cause a
part of the body to move.

EMBRYO RESEARCH

Antonie van Leeuwenhoek studied male and female sex cells under his microscope. However, it took 200 years before the fusion of sperm and egg (fertilization) to form an embryo was actually seen. Today, doctors often use microscopes in their work on artificial fertilization and embryo research. This is necessary since about one in six of adult couples that try to have children fail. Usually it is either because one of the partners does not produce enough sex cells, or the cells are abnormal. Some fertilized egg cells fail to grow and divide into a ball of cells as they should (see left). Much embryo research involves endoscopes – a tube containing a microscope and lighting system that is inserted into the body.

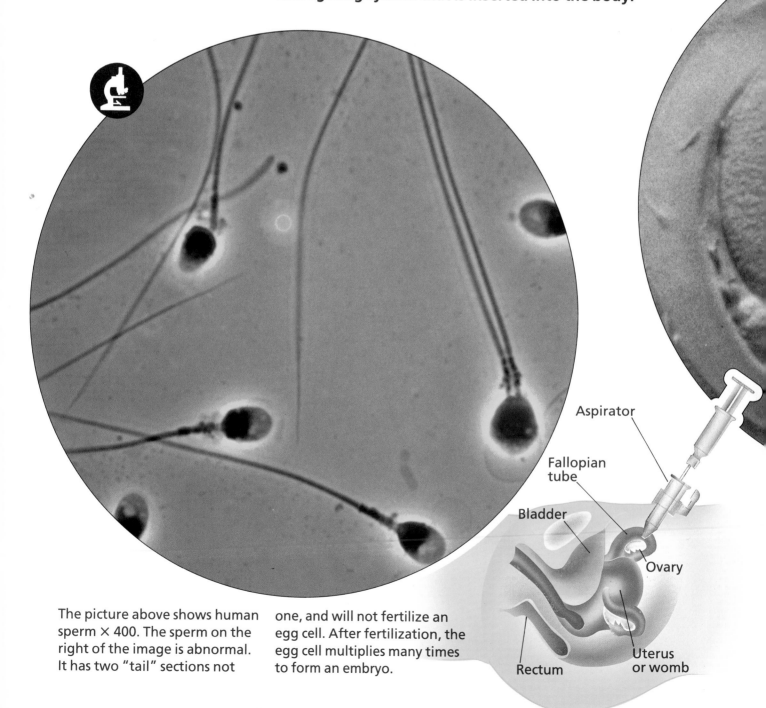

The picture above shows human sperm × 400. The sperm on the right of the image is abnormal. It has two "tail" sections not one, and will not fertilize an egg cell. After fertilization, the egg cell multiplies many times to form an embryo.

Aspirator

Fallopian tube

Bladder

Ovary

Rectum

Uterus or womb

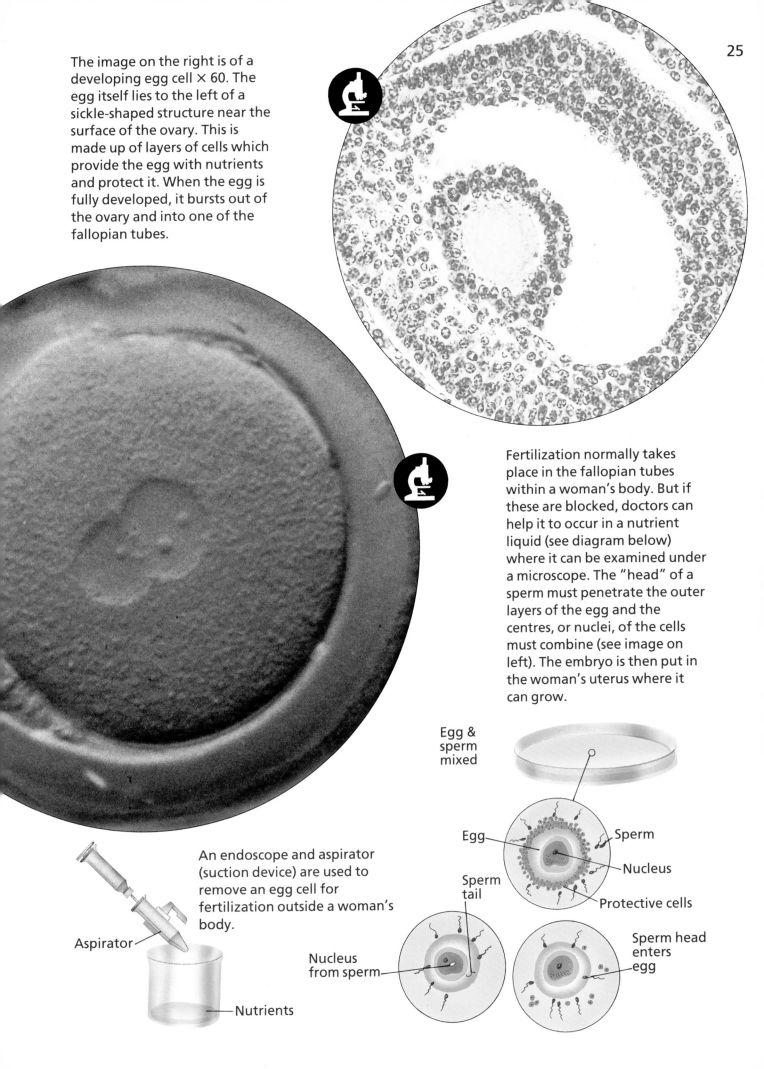

The image on the right is of a developing egg cell × 60. The egg itself lies to the left of a sickle-shaped structure near the surface of the ovary. This is made up of layers of cells which provide the egg with nutrients and protect it. When the egg is fully developed, it bursts out of the ovary and into one of the fallopian tubes.

Fertilization normally takes place in the fallopian tubes within a woman's body. But if these are blocked, doctors can help it to occur in a nutrient liquid (see diagram below) where it can be examined under a microscope. The "head" of a sperm must penetrate the outer layers of the egg and the centres, or nuclei, of the cells must combine (see image on left). The embryo is then put in the woman's uterus where it can grow.

An endoscope and aspirator (suction device) are used to remove an egg cell for fertilization outside a woman's body.

Aspirator

Nutrients

Egg & sperm mixed

Egg

Sperm

Nucleus

Sperm tail

Protective cells

Nucleus from sperm

Sperm head enters egg

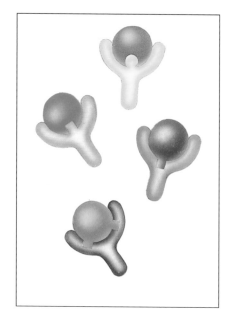

PUTTING MICROBES TO WORK

Many microbes do not cause disease and are helpful to us. The fungi *Pencillium, Streptomyces* and *Aspergillus* produce antibiotics. Many protozoa, algae, fungi and bacteria break down natural substances in sewage and so help cleanse water for drinking. In the past 20 years scientists have used the natural chemical activities of microbes, to make new types of medicines. One microbe in particular, *Escherichia coli* (see top right), has been put to good use. It can be grown and made to produce the hormones and enzymes usually made only by human cells in tiny amounts. Scientists have also used cancer cells from mice to make antibodies, like the ones illustrated below, against harmful microbes.

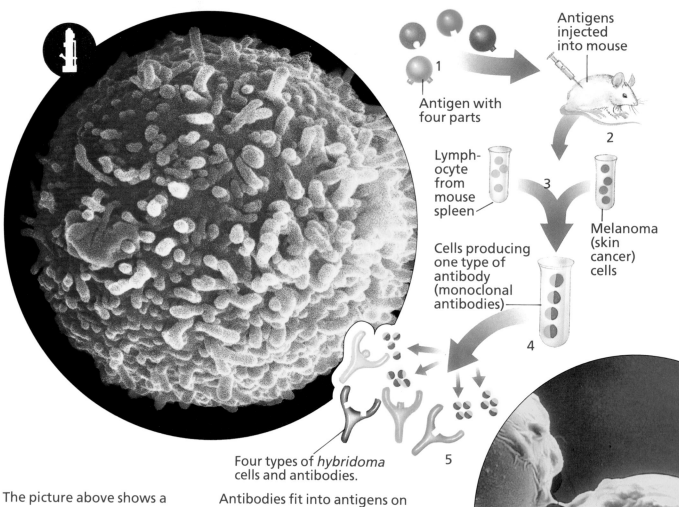

Antigen with four parts

1

Antigens injected into mouse

2

Lymphocyte from mouse spleen

3

Melanoma (skin cancer) cells

Cells producing one type of antibody (monoclonal antibodies)

4

Four types of *hybridoma* cells and antibodies.

5

The picture above shows a *hybridoma* cell magnified × 3000. Unlike ordinary lymphocytes (see page 13) this produces only one type of antibody and, as it multiplies, makes exact copies of itself, called "clones". It can be made to mass-produce antibodies against a bacterium or virus.

Antibodies fit into antigens on the surface of a disease-causing microbe. This *hybridoma* cell was made by joining a white blood cell from a mouse with a mouse's cancer cell. The diagram above shows the five stages in making *hybridoma* cells each producing antibodies against one of the four antigens.

The bacterium *Escherichia coli* (right × 14,700) grows in the human digestive system and usually does no harm. In it is a ring-shaped cell structure called a "chromosome" which contains a series of genes, each producing chemicals needed by the cell. Using other natural chemicals called enzymes, scientists can cut open the chromosome, insert genes from human cells, and then seal it (see below).

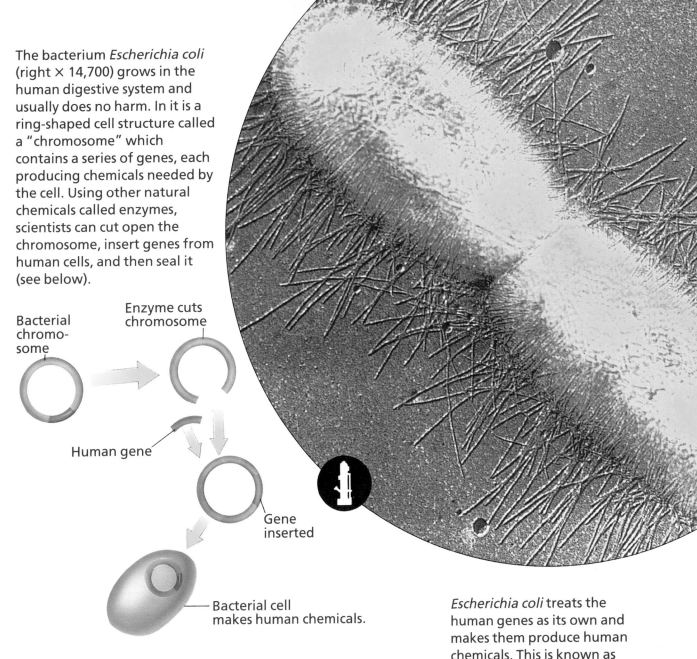

Bacterial chromo-some

Enzyme cuts chromosome

Human gene

Gene inserted

Bacterial cell makes human chemicals.

Escherichia coli treats the human genes as its own and makes them produce human chemicals. This is known as "genetic engineering". Among the useful substances made in this way is interferon, which stops viruses from reproducing and so allows white blood cells to destroy them. It may also combat cancer cells. Human insulin and growth-factor are hormones which some people are unable to make enough of. Producing them by genetic engineering and injecting them into patients helps to solve this problem. The image far left shows cells used for genetic engineering after five hours of growth on tiny glass beads in the laboratory. The image left shows the same cells after 48 hours growth.

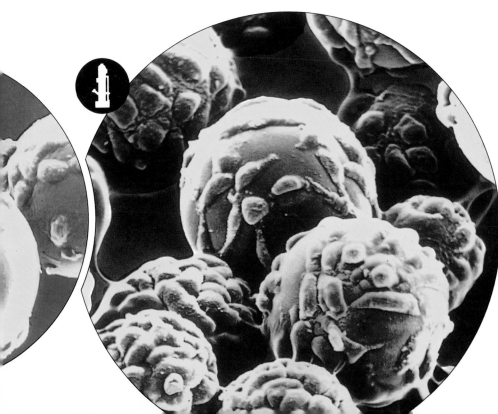

PRACTICAL PROJECTS

You can discover a great deal about how medical scientists work with just a hand lens. But to see greater detail you will need a home microscope like that shown on page 4. The objects you wish to study must be mounted on a glass slide. They must be made thin so that light can shine through them. You may need to cut very thin slices of material or to tease them out until they are very fine. To pick out different types of structures, you will need to stain your specimens. The way to do this is outlined below. If you are going to try something which is a bit tricky, it is worth getting help from an adult. You may be able to start your studies with some ready-made slides bought from a microscope supplier.

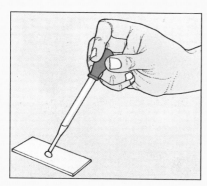

To prepare a slide of cells, place a drop of clean water containing them on the glass.

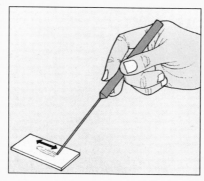

With a wire loop that has been sterilized in a flame, spread the fluid thinly.

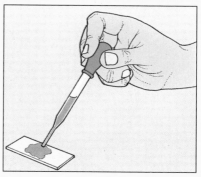

Add a small drop of staining dye to the cells and leave for a few minutes.

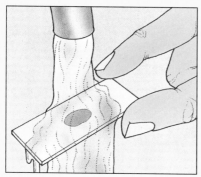

Wash off the dye with water or alcohol. You can stain with another, contrasting dye.

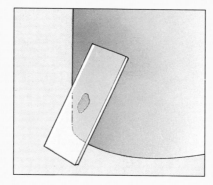

Leave the slide to dry. You can speed up drying by warming the slide over a flame.

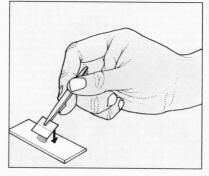

Place the cover slip (a thin square of glass) over the stained cells.

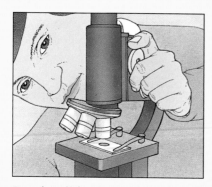

Put the slide on the microscope stage and position the mirror to give you good illumination.

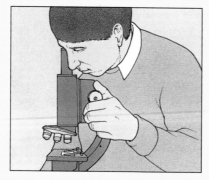

Select the objective lens you want, then move the eyepiece up or down to focus.

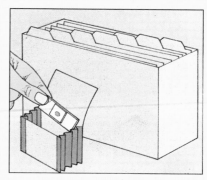

Keep your prepared slides in a cardboard wallet made by folding a thin sheet of card.

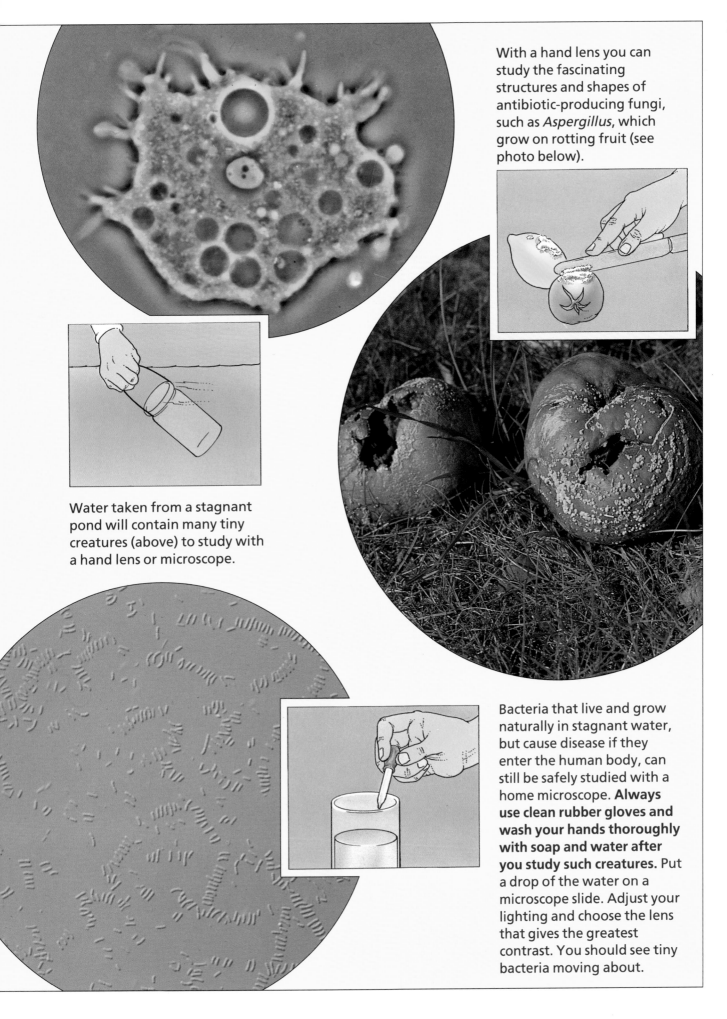

With a hand lens you can study the fascinating structures and shapes of antibiotic-producing fungi, such as *Aspergillus*, which grow on rotting fruit (see photo below).

Water taken from a stagnant pond will contain many tiny creatures (above) to study with a hand lens or microscope.

Bacteria that live and grow naturally in stagnant water, but cause disease if they enter the human body, can still be safely studied with a home microscope. **Always use clean rubber gloves and wash your hands thoroughly with soap and water after you study such creatures.** Put a drop of the water on a microscope slide. Adjust your lighting and choose the lens that gives the greatest contrast. You should see tiny bacteria moving about.

MICROPHOTOGRAPHY

Some of the photographs in this book were taken using a camera with special close-up lenses that magnify the subject in much the same way as a hand-lens would magnify them for your eye. Other images with greater magnifications, like the cancer cells on page 13, were taken by fitting a camera to the eyepiece of a scientific microscope. Such pictures are known as photomicrographs. The colours in these are often those of stains used, rather than natural colours. If you have a home microscope you can take your own photomicrographs. You will need a single lens reflex camera and a special camera attachment. Many images in this book were produced using scanning electron microscopes.

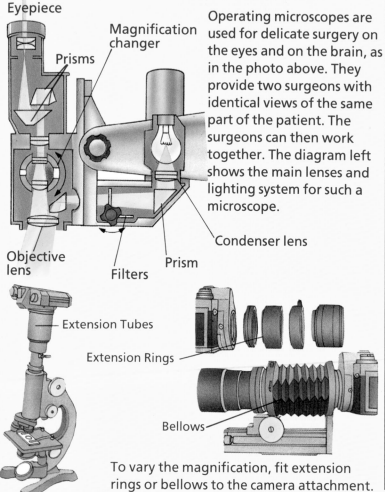

Operating microscopes are used for delicate surgery on the eyes and on the brain, as in the photo above. They provide two surgeons with identical views of the same part of the patient. The surgeons can then work together. The diagram left shows the main lenses and lighting system for such a microscope.

Eyepiece

Magnification changer

Prisms

Objective lens

Filters

Prism

Condenser lens

There are two main types of electron microscope. In a transmission type (TEM), a beam of electrons is passed through an extremely thin slice of tissue and an image is produced on a viewing screen. On a scanning electron microscope (SEM), a fine beam of electrons is moved across the surface of the tissue for reflections to be collected and used to create an image on a television type of screen. Using an SEM, realistic 3-D images are produced and unlike many types of microscope specimens, the creatures can be viewed alive. However, the normal slide preparation process kills live cells. The photos from an SEM have false colours added in processing.

Extension Tubes

Extension Rings

Bellows

To vary the magnification, fit extension rings or bellows to the camera attachment.

GLOSSARY

antibiotic a substance produced by one type of microbe – usually a fungus – that destroys or prevents the growth of another – most commonly a bacterium.

antibody a special type of chemical produced by white blood cells which combat the harmful effects of an antigen.

antigen any substance that the body regards as "foreign" or not part of itself. Antigens include chemicals present on the surface of microbes.

bacteria small single-cell organisms with a cell wall and simple nucleus. They reproduce quickly by splitting in two equal parts. They are neither plants nor animals. Some of them cause diseases in plants and animals.

blood a red fluid that travels around the body in the veins and arteries. It is made up of the plasma, a straw-coloured liquid, in which float red and white cells called corpuscles.

cell one of the building blocks of which living things are made. Some creatures, for example protozoans and bacteria, consist of just one cell. Others, like flowering plants, insects and mammals, are made up of many thousands or millions of cells.

disease an illness with a specific cause and recognizable signs and symptoms. Some diseases are caused by microbes, others by parts of the body not working properly.

enzyme a type of protein produced by the body which speeds up chemical reactions inside cells.

hormones the body's chemical messengers. They flow around the blood system and control tissue growth and development.

infection the invasion of the body by a harmful microbe.

magnification the number of times larger that an object seen through a lens or microscope appears compared with its true size.

microbe any organism or living thing too small to be seen with the naked or unaided eye. Microbes are also known as microorganisms and they include protozoa, bacteria, viruses and some fungi and algae, many of which cause diseases.

neuron a nerve cell. It consists of a long thin fibre and many short root-like projections called the dendrites.

organ a major part of the body such as the heart, lungs, eyes, ears or kidneys. Organs are made up of one or more types of tissue and each organ has a particular job to do.

protozoan a single-celled organism such as the pond creature Amoeba.

tissue a collection of cells of the same type.

virus a tiny organism, too small to be seen with even a home microscope, which can only multiply inside a living cell. Viruses cause changes – diseases – in the 'host' cells and organisms they infect.

WEIGHTS AND MEASURES

mm = millimetres 10mm = 0.4 inch
cm = centimetre 100cm = 1m = 3.3 feet
m = metre 1000m = 1km = 0.6 mile
km = kilometre
lb = pound

g = gram 1000g = 1kg = 2lb 3oz
kg = kilogram
0.1 = 1/10
0.01 = 1/100
0.001 = 1/1000

INDEX

Photographic Credits:
Cover and all the pages up to and including 22: Science Photo Library; page 23 top and bottom: Biophoto Associates; page 24: Science Photo Library; page 25 top: Geoscience Features Library; pages 25 bottom, 25 top and bottom, 27 top and bottom: Science Photo Library; pages 29 top and 29 middle: Biophoto Associates; pages 29 bottom and 30: Science Photo Library.